Becoming a Modern-Day CFO

A Comprehensive Guide to Financial Leadership

Rajendra Choudhary

Table of Contents

1. **Introduction**
   - The Evolving Role of the CFO
   - Purpose of This Book
2. **Chapter 1: The CFO Landscape**
   - Historical Context of the CFO Role
   - The Transition from Traditional to Strategic
   - Key Responsibilities of a Modern CFO
3. **Chapter 2: The Importance of SOPs**
   - Defining Standard Operating Procedures
   - Benefits of SOPs in Financial Management
   - Developing and Implementing Effective SOPs
   - Case Study: Transforming Operations through SOPs
4. **Chapter 3: Embracing Technology in Finance**
   - The Digital Transformation of the CFO Role
   - Essential Technologies for Modern CFOs
   - Automation and Its Impact on Efficiency
   - Data Analytics: Driving Decision-Making
   - Case Study: A CFO's Journey with Technology
5. **Chapter 4: Building Strong Business Partnerships**
   - The CFO as a Strategic Partner
   - Collaborating Across Departments
   - Effective Stakeholder Communication

- Establishing a Culture of Collaboration
- Example: Successful Interdepartmental Projects

6. **Chapter 5: Crafting a Financial Strategy**
    - Setting Financial Goals and Objectives
    - Advanced Budgeting and Forecasting Techniques
    - Risk Management in Financial Strategy
    - Adapting to Market Changes
    - Case Study: Strategic Pivot in Response to Crisis

7. **Chapter 6: Leadership and Team Development**
    - Leading a High-Performing Finance Team
    - Essential Leadership Skills for CFOs
    - Mentorship and Talent Development
    - Fostering a Culture of Continuous Improvement
    - Story: A CFO's Leadership Transformation Journey

8. **Chapter 7: Ethical Considerations and Compliance**
    - The CFO's Role in Governance
    - Understanding Regulatory Requirements
    - Building an Ethical Culture
    - Crisis Management and Response
    - Case Study: Navigating a Compliance Challenge

9. **Chapter 8: Best Practices and Case Studies**
    - Profiles of Successful Modern CFOs
    - Lessons Learned from Their Experiences
    - Best Practices for Effective CFO Leadership

- Story: A Case of Effective Change Management

10.　Chapter 9: The Future of the CFO Role
- Trends Shaping the Future of Finance
- Preparing for Tomorrow's Challenges
- Lifelong Learning and Professional Development

11.　Conclusion
- Recap of Key Insights
- Embracing the Journey as a Modern CFO

12.　References and Further Reading
- Books, Articles, and Resources for Continued Learning

Introduction

The Evolving Role of the CFO

The Chief Financial Officer (CFO) has undergone a significant transformation over the past few decades. Traditionally viewed as the financial steward of an organisation, the modern CFO is a strategic leader and partner who influences business direction and drives innovation. This shift is not merely a trend; it reflects the complex and rapidly changing business environment in which organisations operate today.

Purpose of This Book

This book is designed to provide aspiring CFOs with the knowledge, tools, and insights necessary to excel in this evolving role. We will explore the importance of Standard Operating Procedures (SOPs), technology integration, and effective business partnerships as key components of successful financial leadership. Throughout the book, I will share examples and stories of best practices and transformational journeys that illustrate the principles discussed.

Chapter 1: The CFO Landscape

Historical Context of the CFO Role

The role of the CFO has historically been focused on compliance, reporting, and financial management. In the past, CFOs were primarily concerned with the accuracy of financial statements, ensuring regulatory compliance, and managing budgets. However, as businesses have evolved, so too has the role of the CFO.

The Transition from Traditional to Strategic

Modern CFOs are expected to be strategic partners to the CEO and other executives. They must understand the intricacies of the business, contribute to strategic planning, and provide insights for decision-making. This evolution requires a shift in mindset and skillset for CFOs.

Key Responsibilities of a Modern CFO

1. **Financial Stewardship**: Overseeing financial health and ensuring compliance.
2. **Strategic Planning**: Involvement in long-term strategic initiatives.
3. **Operational Efficiency**: Optimising processes and systems.
4. **Data-Driven Insights**: Utilising analytics for informed decision-making.

Notes:

Chapter 2: The Importance of SOPs

Defining Standard Operating Procedures

Standard Operating Procedures (SOPs) are formalised instructions that dictate how specific tasks should be performed. SOPs help standardise processes, reduce errors, and ensure consistency in financial operations.

Benefits of SOPs in Financial Management

1. **Improved Efficiency**: Streamlined processes lead to time savings.

2. **Consistency and Quality Control**: Ensures uniformity in financial reporting.

3. **Knowledge Retention**: Preserves institutional knowledge amidst employee turnover.

4. **Enhanced Compliance**: Ensures adherence to regulatory requirements.

Developing and Implementing Effective SOPs

1. **Identify Key Processes**: Focus on critical areas that impact the organisation. For eg. AP, AR, GL, Tax, Master data management, procurement, credit policy etc.

2. **Collaborate with Stakeholders**: Involve team members in the creation process.

3. **Draft Clear Instructions**: Create step-by-step procedures that are easy to follow.

4. **Train Employees**: Ensure all relevant staff are trained on new SOPs.

Case Study: Transforming Operations through SOPs

Consider the case of ABC Corp, which faced challenges in its financial reporting process. The CFO implemented SOPs that standardised the reporting timeline, outlined data collection procedures, and established clear roles. As a result, the company reduced reporting time by 40%, minimised errors, ensured consistency, and enhanced stakeholder confidence.

Notes:

Chapter 3: Embracing Technology in Finance

The Digital Transformation of the CFO Role

The digital transformation has fundamentally altered how CFOs operate. Technology plays a crucial role in streamlining processes, improving accuracy, and providing insights that drive strategic decisions.

Essential Technologies for Modern CFOs

1. **Cloud Computing**: Enables real-time access to financial data.
2. **Enterprise Resource Planning (ERP) Systems**: Integrates various business functions into one platform.
3. **Business Intelligence (BI) Tools**: Offers data visualisation and analysis capabilities.
4. **Artificial Intelligence (AI)**: Automates repetitive tasks and enhances forecasting.

Automation and Its Impact on Efficiency

Automation of routine tasks allows finance teams to focus on more strategic activities. For example, automating invoice processing can significantly reduce manual errors and processing times. Identifying these tasks and outsourcing them is a first step in this.

Data Analytics: Driving Decision-Making

Modern CFOs must leverage data analytics to gain insights into financial performance. By analysing historical data, CFOs can identify trends, forecast future performance, and support strategic initiatives.

Case Study: A CFO's Journey with Technology

ABC Industries implemented an AI-driven analytics platform that transformed its financial forecasting process. The CFO reported a 50%

improvement in forecasting accuracy, allowing the company to make more informed strategic decisions and allocate resources effectively.

Notes:

Chapter 4: Building Strong Business Partnerships

The CFO as a Strategic Partner

To thrive, CFOs must cultivate relationships across the organisation. This collaboration enables them to understand different perspectives and align financial strategies with broader business objectives.

Collaborating Across Departments

1. **Engage with Other Leaders**: Regularly meet with department heads to discuss their needs and challenges.
2. **Align Financial and Operational Goals**: Ensure that financial strategies support overall business objectives.
3. **Facilitate Cross-Functional Teams**: Encourage collaboration on projects that require diverse expertise.

Effective Stakeholder Communication

CFOs must effectively communicate financial information to non-financial stakeholders. This includes presenting complex data in a digestible format and highlighting its implications for business strategy.

Establishing a Culture of Collaboration

Foster a culture of collaboration within the finance team and across the organisation. Encourage open communication and joint problem-solving to enhance business performance.

Example: Successful Interdepartmental Projects

Consider the collaboration between the finance and sales departments at DEF Corp. By working together on a pricing policy, the CFO helped the sales team to have visibility of historical product pricing and costing. This led to increase in the profit by 10%.

Notes:

Chapter 5: Crafting a Financial Strategy

Setting Financial Goals and Objectives

A successful financial strategy starts with clear, measurable goals aligned with the organisation's overall mission. CFOs should ensure these goals are communicated and understood throughout the organisation.

Advanced Budgeting and Forecasting Techniques

1. **Zero-Based Budgeting**: Requires justification for all expenses, promoting efficiency.
2. **Rolling Forecasts**: Updates forecasts regularly to reflect changing business conditions.
3. **Scenario Planning**: Prepares for various market conditions by developing multiple financial scenarios.

Risk Management in Financial Strategy

Effective risk management is crucial for sustaining financial health. CFOs should:

1. **Identify Risks**: Regularly evaluate potential risks to the organisation.
2. **Establish Internal Controls**: Implement procedures to mitigate risks associated with financial reporting.
3. **Develop Crisis Management Plans**: Prepare for potential crises with well-defined response strategies.

Adapting to Market Changes

CFOs must remain agile and ready to adjust financial strategies in response to market dynamics. Continuous monitoring of industry trends and economic indicators is essential.

Case Study: Strategic Pivot in Response to Crisis

During the COVID-19 pandemic, GHI Corp's CFO led the organisation through a strategic pivot. By analysing cash flow projections and adapting the budget, the company not only survived but also identified new growth opportunities, resulting in a 20% increase in revenue by the end of the fiscal year.

Notes:

Chapter 6: Leadership and Team Development

Leading a High-Performing Finance Team

Effective leadership is critical for building a high-performing finance team. CFOs should create an environment that encourages collaboration, innovation, and accountability.

Essential Leadership Skills for CFOs

1. **Emotional Intelligence**: Understanding and managing emotions to foster positive relationships.
2. **Strategic Thinking**: Ability to see the big picture and make informed decisions.
3. **Effective Communication**: Clearly convey ideas and expectations to team members.

Mentorship and Talent Development

Investing in team members' professional development is vital for retaining talent and ensuring organisational success. CFOs should provide mentorship, training opportunities, and pathways for advancement. Monthly open forum meetings and annual off-site seminars can be first step in this.

Fostering a Culture of Continuous Improvement

Encourage a mindset of continuous improvement within the finance team. Solicit feedback, promote ongoing learning, and celebrate successes to enhance team performance.

Story: A CFO's Leadership Transformation Journey

JKL Corp's CFO faced challenges in team morale and productivity. By implementing regular team-building activities, mentorship programs, and transparent communication, he transformed the finance team into a cohesive, high-performing unit, leading to a 25% increase in efficiency and reduction in employee turnover.

Notes:

Chapter 7: Ethical Considerations and Compliance

The CFO's Role in Governance

CFOs play a critical role in maintaining governance and ethical standards within the organisation. They should promote transparency and accountability in all financial practices.

Understanding Regulatory Requirements

CFOs must stay informed about relevant regulations and compliance requirements. This includes financial reporting standards, tax laws, and industry-specific regulations.

Building an Ethical Culture

Promote an ethical culture within the finance team and the broader organisation. Lead by example and establish clear policies regarding ethical behaviour.

Crisis Management and Response

Prepare for potential crises by developing a crisis management plan that outlines procedures for communication, decision-making, and recovery.

Case Study: Navigating a Compliance Challenge

When MNO Corp faced a regulatory audit, the CFO proactively implemented a compliance training program for the finance team. This initiative not only helped navigate the audit successfully but also reinforced a culture of compliance and accountability throughout the organisation.

Notes:

Chapter 8: Best Practices and Case Studies

Profiles of Successful Modern CFOs

Highlighting the careers of notable CFOs who have successfully navigated the challenges of the role can provide valuable insights. These leaders have demonstrated adaptability, strategic thinking, and the ability to foster collaboration.

Lessons Learned from Their Experiences

Identify common themes and best practices from the careers of successful CFOs. These insights can guide aspiring CFOs in their professional development.

Best Practices for Effective CFO Leadership

1. **Embrace Change**: Be willing to adapt and evolve as the business landscape shifts.

2. **Invest in Technology**: Leverage technology to improve efficiency and decision-making.

3. **Foster Collaboration**: Build strong relationships across the organisation to drive success.

Story: A Case of Effective Change Management

PQR Ltd. underwent a significant restructuring, and the CFO played a crucial role in managing the transition. By effectively communicating the reasons for the change and engaging employees throughout the process, the CFO minimised resistance and successfully implemented the new organisational structure.

Notes:

Chapter 9: The Future of the CFO Role

Trends Shaping the Future of Finance

The landscape of finance continues to evolve. Trends such as remote work, increased reliance on data analytics, and a focus on sustainability are reshaping the CFO role.

Preparing for Tomorrow's Challenges

CFOs must remain adaptable and proactive in addressing emerging challenges. This includes investing in new technologies, understanding market dynamics, and fostering a culture of innovation.

Lifelong Learning and Professional Development

To remain effective, CFOs must commit to continuous learning and professional development. Staying informed about industry trends, best practices, and new technologies will be essential for future success.

Notes:

Conclusion

Recap of Key Insights

The modern CFO plays a critical role in shaping organisational strategy and driving financial performance. By embracing technology, establishing strong SOPs, and fostering business partnerships, CFOs can navigate the complexities of today's business environment.

Embracing the Journey as a Modern CFO

The journey to becoming a modern CFO is ongoing. Embrace the challenges and opportunities that come your way, and remain committed to continuous improvement, learning, and leadership.

Notes:

References and Further Reading

- **Books**:
    - "CFO Techniques: A Hands-on Guide to Financial Management"
    - "The CFO Guidebook" by Steven M. Bragg
- **Articles**:
    - Relevant articles from Harvard Business Review, CFO Magazine, and industry publications.
- **Online Resources**:
    - Webinars, courses, and forums for ongoing professional development.

This comprehensive guide provides aspiring CFOs with the tools, strategies, and insights needed to thrive in the evolving landscape of financial leadership. By focusing on SOPs, technology, and collaboration, you can position yourself as a key driver of success within your organisation.

www.ingramcontent.com/pod-product-compliance
Lightning Source LLC
Chambersburg PA
CBHW032312240526
45464CB00023BA/2993